Storm Window

By RL Lane

"The storm that comes just once in a lifetime…it is the only one you don't have to run and hide from…" RL Lane

It is coincidentally one of the stormiest summers. The Farmer's Almanac got it right. Storm after storm after storm…

Lighting

Thunder

Rain hail

Hail the rain they used to say

It was like a God by itself

The natives would look up…eyes questioning

Why? When will you fall again?

If we pray, chant will you come back sooner

If we look the other way

Will you come out to play

If we forget about you

Will you go away…

That is not the introduction I was expecting. Although I knew this book was going to have an important message. "This final art book". For now. I need to stop writing. I need a break. I told them I will do just this last one. Plus, I really want to do "EcarreT" just because I love the name. Maybe I am not supposed to. Would it be confusing if a book was named that because it is also the series name for the books? I guess it would be confusing. There is enough confusion in this world. I am trying to get to the un-confusion…

Sort it all out

Un-jumble

Un-mess

Let it lie there in a heap

Many things hidden on the bottom

Like my dirty clothes

Stuff them in the hamper

Keep on putting more and more things on top

Push them down harder until we can fit no more

We no longer fit?

Did we create a world where we

No longer fit…

I already drew the pictures. The first is on your cover…

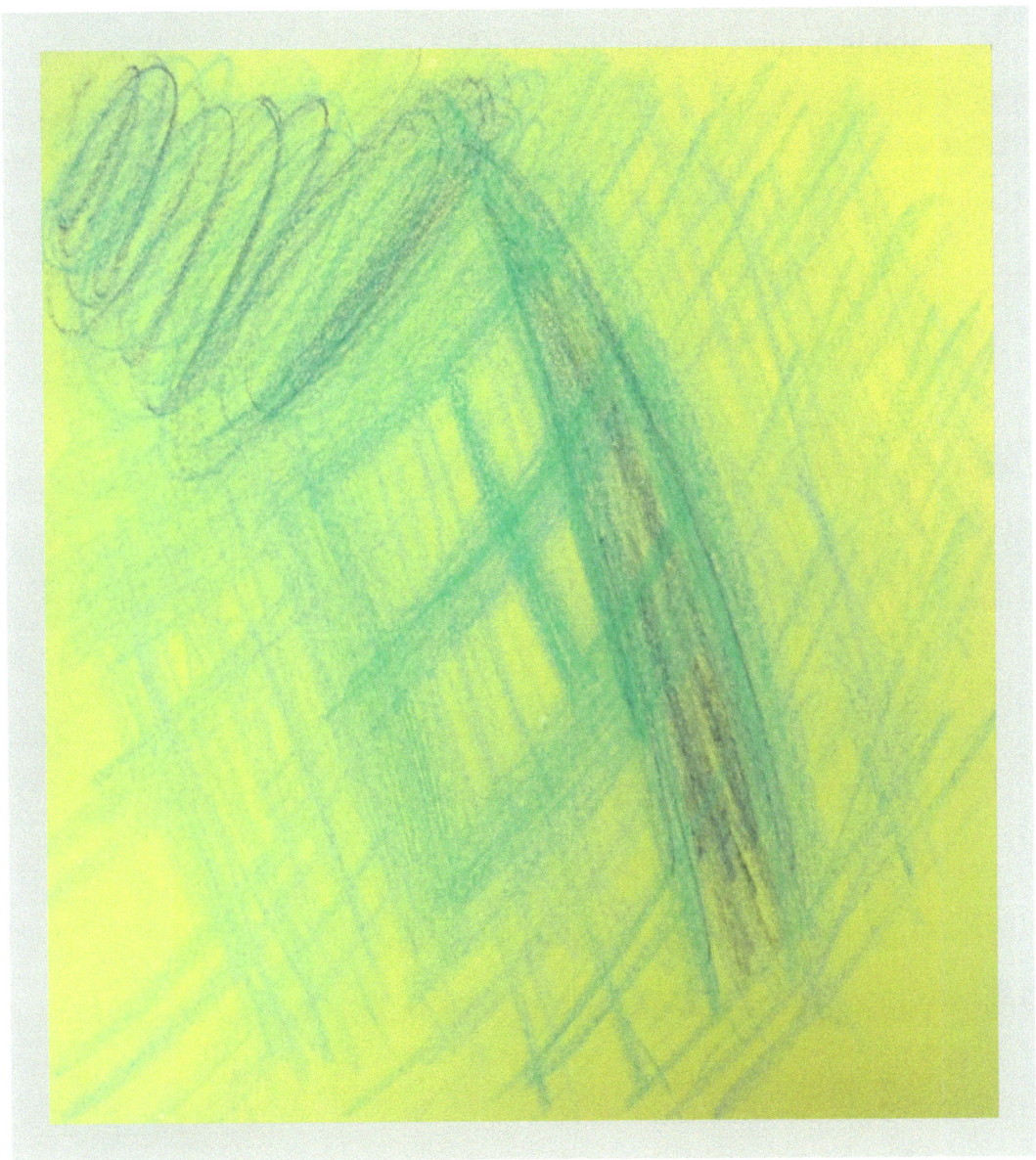

It reminds me of tornado rain gushing down. Why is the rain two colors? Is it really RL Lane rushing in to save the day? Her scarf hanging down…

She is running around in a whirl

Jumping around

From one topic to the next

Some of the books are hard to read

Emotionally and mentally

They are probably not what you want to read on vacation

Or are they what you want to read?

I really have no idea yet

However, I do know there are two of you out there

In the UK

I have been meaning to write about you but kept forgetting

You reading my words

Has brought light to my days

I am not really sure why

I am so excited about you two

Maybe you are friends

Maybe one found me first and you told the other

Maybe you just like the drawings…

This is the other picture I drew for this book…

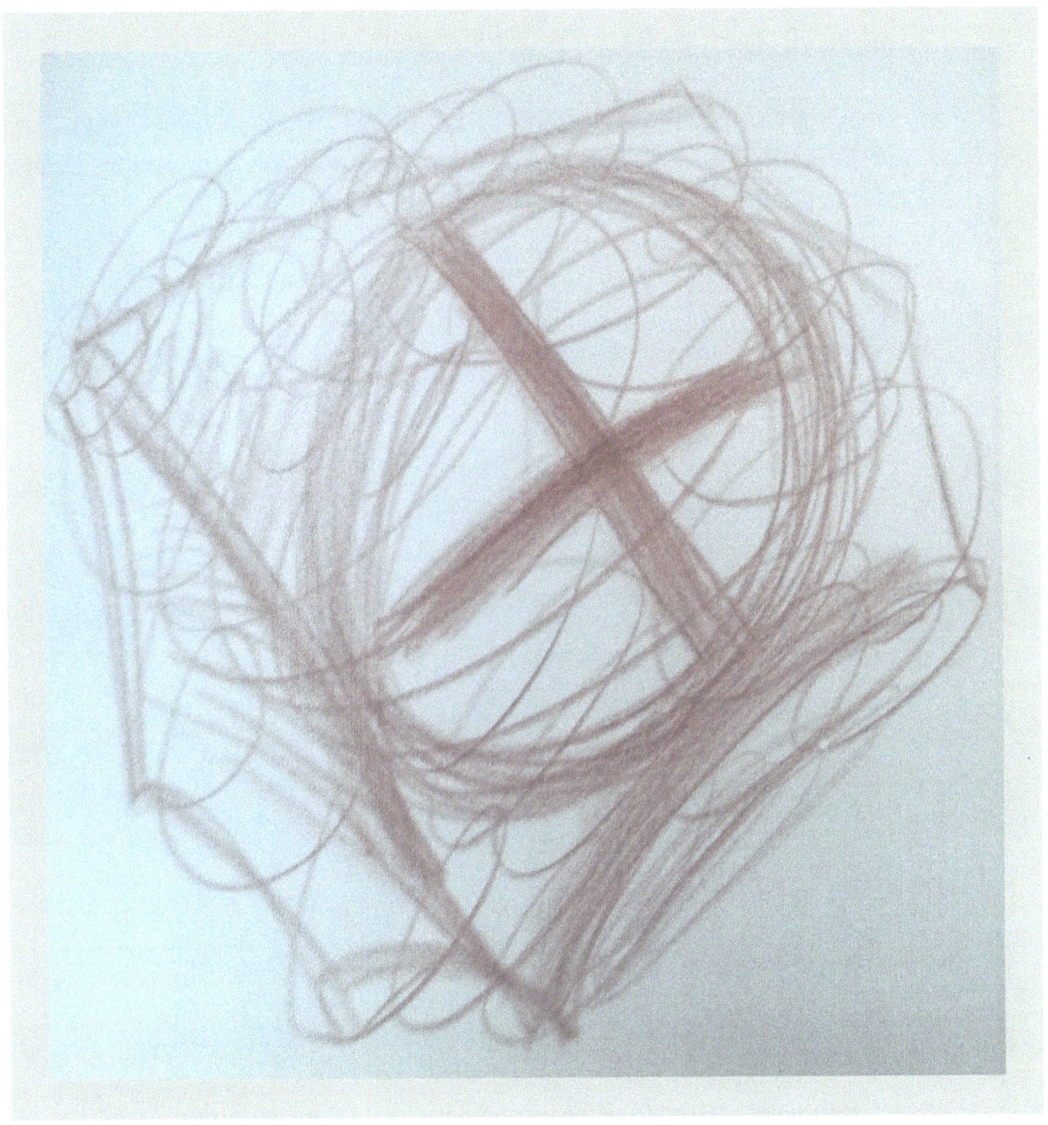

Once I got done, I knew right away that it was the ship window. The Doctor's ship. USS LST 494. The Navy. WWII. You can easily see the wood cross in the window…

I have no doubt he prayed there

As the ship tossed and turned

Bounced along the waves

What did he really see when he looked out that window?

Port window

What did he see?

He says he saw things he didn't want to see

That is a cop-out right?

That is why he never spoke about it

Just like the others

Don't speak about it…like we just said…

If we forget about you

Will you go away…

What they saw…would it go away if they tried to forget about what they saw…

About the Author and *Illustrator*

RL Lane has published the EcarreT series and a collection of art books featuring the illustrations throughout the books. The series begins with "Chapel Street Signs"…

…unexplained connections that challenge us to beli ve. A woman, a Dad a Doctor, a cat and mouse, a horse and tale tell their stories. "Do you beli ve in spirits?" I asked my friend. "Well look", he said, "I believe there are things that cannot be explained…" Oh. Plus, hear ov a Mom's battle with her struggle to connect to the woman…her little girl.

Welcome to EcarreT…a world
Where everyone cares
Why did I have to create it in…

A fiction fantasy world?

You may already know why, but you will see regardless of what you believe as a girl's journey of love and faith on her "Touring Machine" take her on the best journey of her mundane life. A life well on its way takes a turn in a direction that could've never been seen or even dreamed…

The author can be contacted at:

RosaLeeeLane@gmail.com
www.Amazon.com/author/readrllane

I left it in the middle of the book instead of at the end. The "About the Author and *Illustrator*". Illustrator is in italics. It is so important to me. I am in the middle. It is so important to me. The middle child. That should be obvious to all by now...

I had to finally take the last step to

Become RL Lane

I had to look like her...

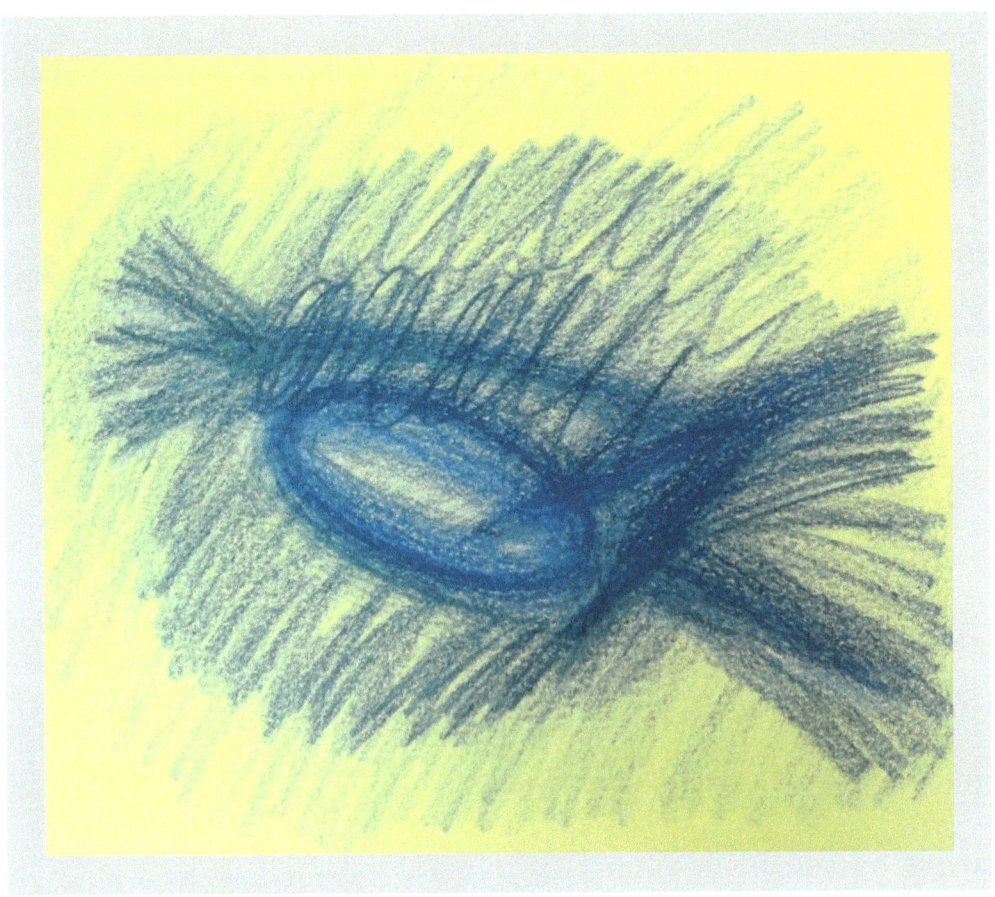

The tweezers came out. The hair clippers too. Then the dye.

I stared at this picture for a long time

Turned it all around

I am missing something about it

What am I supposed to see?

I still have two eyes. I am not Cyclops

The picture fades away the further you get from the center

Why?

The further we get from the truth

The more obscure we become?

Obscure – not discovered or known about. That is me.

When I turn it a certain way, I can glimpse the

Little girl's pigtails

The brush winding around

Her mom did always like her in curls

She had straight straight hair

It is a blue eye

I forgot to tell you my Dad had two blue eyes

Before he lost sight in the one eye. He had blue eyes

That is what got recorded on his military service records

I thought he had green eyes

The one without sight turned green as an adult

So he had one green and one blue eye

Is that what this is about?

He has back his one blue eye now

The one that had no sight for all those years

He has his sight

Back now

His green eye is blue once again…he can see once again…he no longer has to worry about his one good eye because now he has

Two good eyes again

To see it all

From the other side...

Wasn't this book supposed to have some great epiphany? Something we haven't realized until now? Why is RL lane…Lane done writing? Why why why? Does she need to go down another lane? Is there another path she is supposed to follow now? The art? Is it the art? Can she do something else with it?

I honestly don't know. It is not writer's block. I could keep on writing is…if I wanted to but I am supposed to stop. I feel like I am supposed to stop. Why? What am I waiting for? I honestly have no idea…

It is so odd. Never in my life have I felt this way. What is coming next? They said recently that the dresses are important. I had designed some clothing. Are one of you readers looking for a fashion designer? I doubt that is it.

I did just see George last night. He was a famous American comedian. Did you know he was born in January, like my Dad? Oh my gosh! He was born in 1896! He died in 1964! Another person who died before I was even born. I had no idea! Those televisions kept him alive as if he still walked this earth. Oh wait. That is wrong. He died in 1996. That is so odd. My eyes saw 1964 when I looked him up online. Wait! 1964 is important. His wife died in 1964. Not even 40 years old. George made it to 100 years. He just made it by a couple of months. I have no doubt he waited to go. Oh wait. His wife was older than 40. She was 69 when she died. The same age as my Dad. The dates I first looked at were the dates they were married. She had a lot of first names, but everyone knew her as Gracie. Both of their children have already passed away.

I have no idea where we are going with this…

Who else just came up? Mr. Hawthorne did last night as well.
Oh and Johnny. Mr. Carson and George did know each other. I am
scared. What are they trying to say? Mr. Hawthorne died before either
of them were ever born. Did you know he was born on the 4th of July in
Salem, MA? He was of course an American novelist and short story
writer. Wait! Is this what he wants? Do they want me to write short
stories now? I could if they want…

Oh my gosh! No! This is what he wanted me to say…

His uncle!

His ancestors include John Hathorne. He was the only judge
involved in the famous Salem witch trials who never repented of his
actions! Nathaniel added the "w" to make his last name "Hawthorne"
to hide his relation to the judge!

That is what he…we had to uncover!

He can have his redemption now!

I am a witch and I forgive you Judge Hathorne.

Did you think you were making the right decision at the time?
You didn't have all the information we do today. Was there pressure
from others? There were a lot of people afraid of witches back then.
There are still people afraid of witches. Or did you lead others to
believe the women were witches. You were so adamant that you were
right and they were wrong.

He was a strong man. Be a man. Be a man. Take care of it all
for us. The weaker will hide behind you and be the first to criticize if
you make the wrong decisions. He did stand up for what he believed.
There is no doubt about that. Did you know he followed in his dad's
footsteps and was involved in the colonial military? He had to be a
strong man to lead forces. Spiritual or otherwise…

Peace for Nathaniel's great-great grandfather.

Short stories…here we come. How long do they have to be? I consider these books my "adult children's books". The first short story…what shall you be called? Oh. The Christmas one will be "Bells to Believe".

Johnny and George, I am still not sure what you need. I have no doubt we'll figure it out. Does that rhyme?

I remembered that I had started "Whose Tooth", but never finished it. I think it just belongs here. This was the front cover...

Whose Tooth?

A book by RL Lane

This was the back cover…

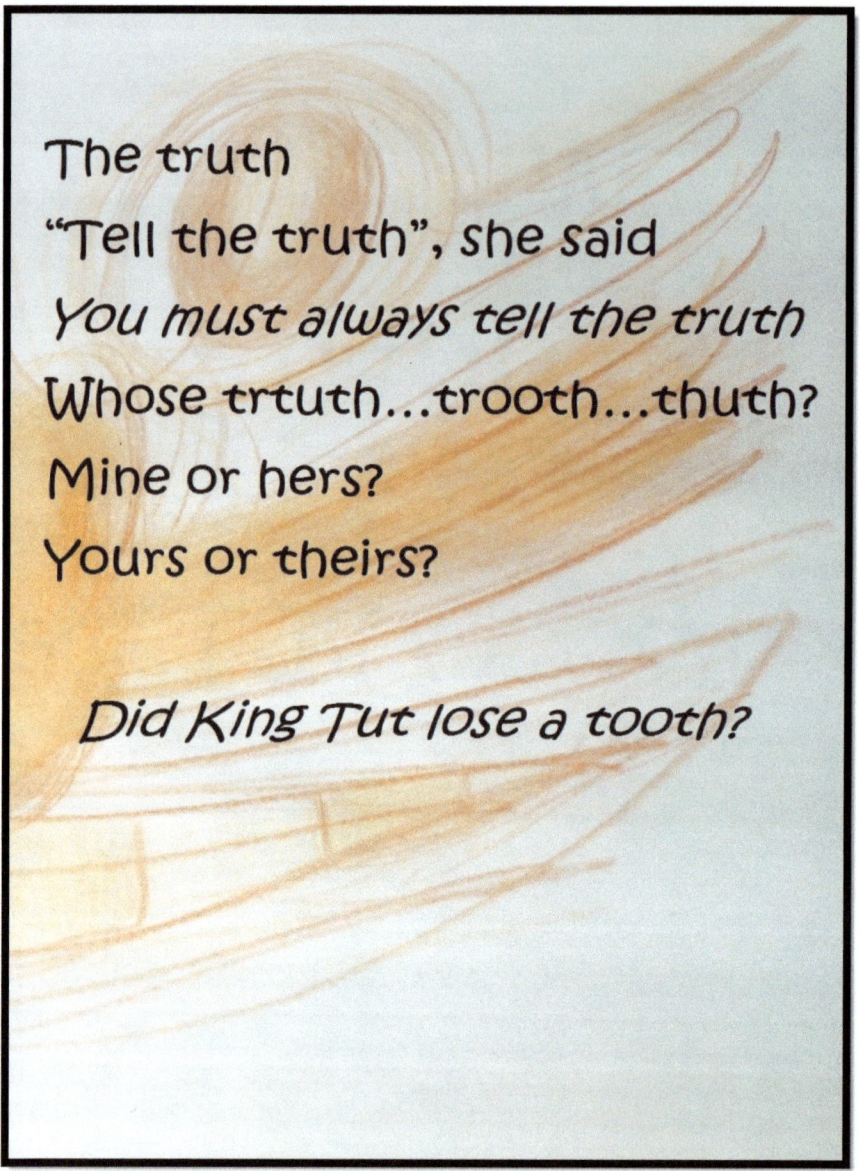

The truth
"Tell the truth", she said
You must always tell the truth
Whose trtuth…trooth…thuth?
Mine or hers?
Yours or theirs?

Did King Tut lose a tooth?

I didn't realize it until I read it out loud that the line with the "thuth" in it sounds like a person talking with a missing front tooth.

Here is the whole picture…

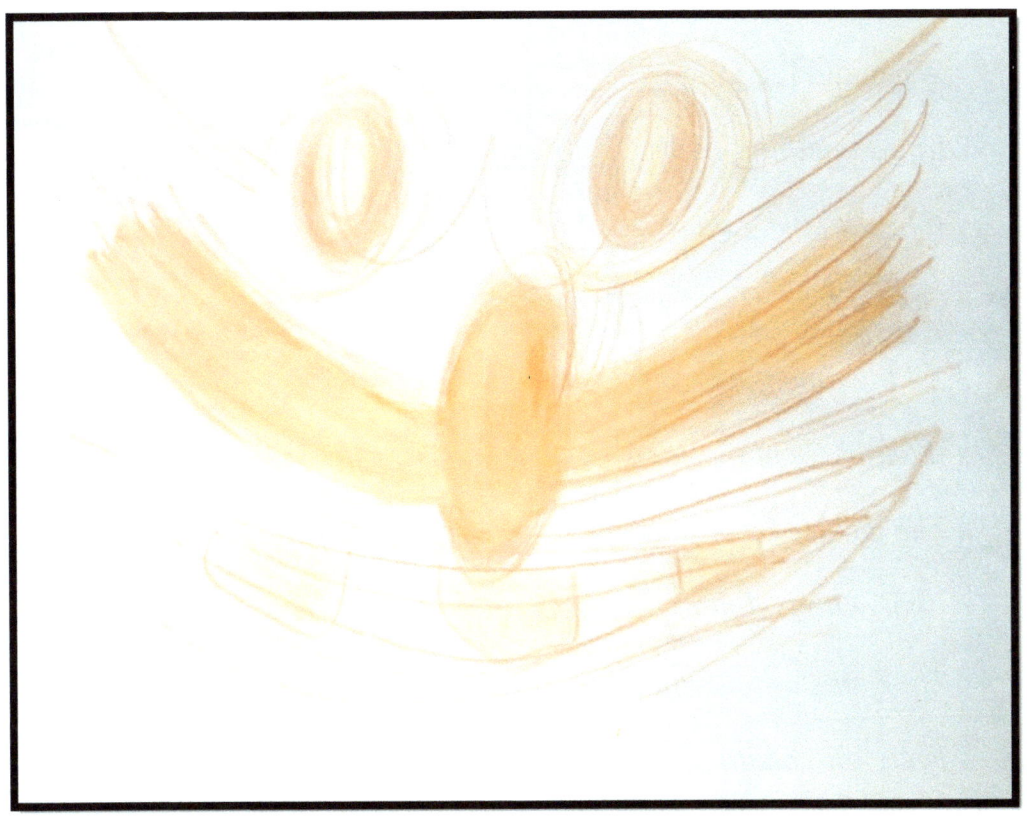

Something about this makes me think of George. Did Mr. Burns have the orange cat and not Bob? Did someone draw Mr. Burns as an orange cat caricature? Did they name the picture King Tut? Why is the middle front tooth that shape? It must

Mean

Something

What?

Does it mean

Have I just showed you the dangerous game to play as a writer…write and wonder…dream and imagine…

When did it *change?*

Into something that was no longer fiction

When do the games we play

Go too far?

All the time

We take them too far…

The game of an affair

Ends with a shot to the head

The game of bullying

Ends with a suicide

The game of drinking

Ends with an overdose

    The game of monopoly

    Ends when you are bankrupt

    Then what?

    What happens when the game ends?

    What are you left with?

You are left with everything.

What you lost was nothing

You were just playing a game

It wasn't real

What you won and what you lost were never yours

They were only in your head

An imagination

So imagine this…

You are going along in a mundane life

And one day you are not

Well, you are still going along

But something happened

You can see the world for the first time

You can do things that you could never do before

Of course you would wonder why did this happen

Of course you would try to find an answer

But whatever the answer is it really doesn't matter

Just keep going along…

You really never know what tomorrow will bring…

Short story world…here we come…

I feel like "Johnny and George" is supposed to be the title of the first one...or is it "Johnny and Gorge"?

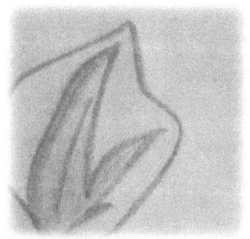

www.ingramcontent.com/pod-product-compliance
Lightning Source LLC
Chambersburg PA
CBHW050911180526
45159CB00007B/2874